Karen Ann Tepperis:

AF220401

"Leopard Lady"

Karen Ann Tepperis

Leopard Lady

Poetry

Bibliografische Information der Deutschen
Nationalbibliothek:
Die Deutsche Nationalbibliothek verzeichnet diese
Publikation in der Deutschen Nationalbibliografie;
detaillierte bibliografische Daten sind im Internet über
http://dnb.dnb.de abrufbar.

Zeichnung: Karen Ann Tepperis

Herstellung und Verlag: BoD – Books on Demand,
Norderstedt

ISBN: 978-3-7519-7118-8

I dedicate this book to my family: husband Gerhard, sons Stephen and Daniel, daughter-in-law Nina, and grandchildren Emily, Elias and Lennard.

Content

Preface

The title of the book, "Leopard Lady", seemed a natural title for me to choose. Through the years I have accumulated a collection of clothes and accessories with a leopard pattern - jackets, trousers, skirts, shoes, boots, scarves, hats, tights, and even a pair of glasses with matching etui. There is a special poem too called Leopard Lady.

During my writing phases I often woke up in the night to jot down verses and ideas that came to mind. I would put pen and paper in various places in the house so that I could write down notes at any given moment before those thoughts left my mind.

The verses often came spontaneously and at all times of day or night. I sometimes had to leave the dinner table to write down a thought quickly. My husband bought me a dictaphone so that on walks, I could dictate any new thoughts.

Themes of my poetry are diverse. They range from my cat, Edgar (Eddie, Mick), Christmas trees, A trip to Texas, A fish called Ronald, my two sons, my two breasts, my singing on the stage, the

English cook Jamie Oliver, to an important theme for me - messies, to mention just some.

Karen Ann Tepperis 2020

1 KATHY AND HER CHRISTMAS TREES

Friday 16th Jan. 2009

In Texas, on an English Studies trip. Kathy, an English teacher lives on a ranch which also has Christmas trees.

If you see a snake, she said, you'll be dead
If you don't chop it in two – like I do.
She saw my shocked face, I fear –
I don't think I'll do that, my dear!
You're in Texas now, a gruesome place
She said to me, it has to be.
Can't afford to feel so fussily.

So there I was – chopping snakes and cutting trees
Rather wobbly at the knees,
What if something just goes wrong
Before I finish up this song,
And chop my foot or something else.

I really do not care for this,
Not my idea of winter bliss.
Tricky trees and slimy snakes,
Not to mention my back-aches.

Oh Kathy, chop the trees alone,
To other things may I be prone.
Like sipping winter warming tea,

Snowball fun, jollity

Don't scorn if I don't come up to hope.
I'll sell the trees! With décor too!
Bangles, baubles, stars and stripes.
A special tree for every type.
Pink and silver gold and white
Twinkling starlets ever bright.

This is my meteor, I am sure
Artistic touch to every tree
Bringing back some hope for me
I'll sell your trees till all be gone
They'll love the look I give them all
Bright and brilliant, big and tall
Fat and funny, fine and small.
All the trees a gem will be
Waiting for their family.
Christmas spent in such a crowd
Makes you want to sing out loud
Hallelujah way up on high
Kathy, when the folks come by
They'll see the trees and want to buy
A big one, full of golden dust
Bows and trinkets, in God we trust
That all the trees be sold at last
Then we go home, so fast

Tearing home for turkey, tea and Christmas pud.
Celebrating as we should.

Singing carols, feeling fine,
Giving presents so divine.
Oh, don't forget to drink some wine.
A Christmas treat you now will see
For Kathy and her Christmas tree.

Kathy says: "Tree sales were good,
Despite the economic crunch."
She lights one up for all the kids
With a pretty pot of punch.

2 UNDER the MULBERRY TREE

Jan.   2009

Under the Mulberry Tree
In the garden
Lynn and Sharon lying in the hammock
Licking lollies

There came a bee.
Struggles to get out of that hammock.
I, the eldest, laughing

At them
Tumbling, fumbling
To see the bee
Under the tree
In the garden.

3 MARCH IS HERE

Longing now for green and Spring
Yearning just to let it in.
See the sprouting jumping shoots
Rise above their baby roots
Growing (sprouting) high and feel at ease
Touch of slightly summer breeze
Long for all the warmth in me
Come right out and hug that tree
Leaves and buds and shrubs and sprouts
Got to let it all hang out

In the springing stratosphere
Dancing daffodils so dear
Other flowers also here
Yellow as the dawn lit day

Wrapped in yellow looking hay
Will it ever go away in autumn
When the sky is grey?
No, not now is said, it's March

March is swooming round our head
Bathed in blossom,
Nothing dead
Blue and white, lilac, red.
Flying high it must be said

Gazing at the forest sky

Seeing tulips wobbling high
What a day to celebrate!
Can't be bad, no one to hate.
A smile, a joke a friendly fate
Walking up and down the wood
Spring is here –
Is understood.

4 WHITNEY

A Journey with their teacher, Mrs. Tepperis, from
Frankfurt to Washington, then on to Texas, to visit
teacher Kathy and school in Whitney, Texas. (N.B.
Washington, unfortunately, has 3 airports!)

What, we are NOT there!
Then, where?
I do not know,
But not THERE

Where we should be
The problem is
We didn't see
The coach driver
Drive us to the wrong airport
(Washington Airport) 1, 2, or 3?
We took for granted
He should know –
That American driver
Experience galore
But he didn't know
Much more than us
As it be, stuck! We three, or five,
No, we numbered more
18 in all, almost a score
Of teenagers
Though old, when they did see
We were off the track

Not so easy to get back.
Tears were trickling - And I, I had to see
Things put right as quick as be

My first trick was to send the lot
Into the scrumptious burger shop
There they all did trot
Inside to sip a coke, or two
Pop a pie into their mouths
While I did see what I could do.
I saw a trickling tear, or two,
From girls so big   so I was strong
The day was young and there was lots to do
To quick get done. The passports here
The passports there
I know I really have to care.
I wonder if I'll ever hear
The last plane call to Whitney clear.

To risk the ride to Airport 2
To catch our plane
Not Tim-buk-two!
We had to go to Texas – straight
Our ride was urgent
Don't be late
To get to Chicago, would be great
Then onward bound
Into Texas – Kathy ground.

Whitney was to be our spot

Got the kids, passports, The lot.
And the money for the ride
From airport one
To airport two
A costly game,
Forget the view
We never had the time for fun,
We grabbed our cases,
Had to run!
To be in time
Chicago land
Speeding on, hand in hand
Only minutes, we made it though
Creeping on the plane, tip-toe
Sitting back, a breath so deep –
Time just for a little sleep.

Arrived in Whitney, A deadly hour,
Wanting just to take a shower.
Kathy there, she wasn't late,
With hoards of kids, so kind, sedate.
She passed the coffee all around
Nice and frothy, not a sound.
The kids were tired, all worn out,
When suddenly, there came a shout!
Kathy saw me, I'm her mate,
She cuddled me, oh kiss me Kate!

5 WHEN I SING UPON A STAGE

16.01.09   22:00h Evening

When I sing upon a stage
Forget my sadness
And my age
Blossom out in other lands
Hear the music of the band
Raise my brows,
And breathe in deep
Let the power flow and seep
Flowing hair and waving arms
Presenting people
All my charms

Whacking out in one great stab
A song of love, a song of cheer
A whiff of wine, or bubbly beer
Sentiments to warm and slide
To memories that often hide
All feeling deep, all fate and woe.
Where did our emotion go?

I find it only on the stage
A therapy, a seminar
No time now to hum and ha.
Just sing it out, don't hold it in
If only life was just as thin –
Uncomplicated, there's no doubt –
In life you cannot sing it out.
There's here an "ah", and there an "oh!"

And "oh I don't believe you" – so

I sing it on the stage
Feeling somewhat in a cage
The audience they stare at me
Is it all unnaturally?
Standing there, in dresses grand
Wanting them to understand
I sing although it wasn't planned
Won't somebody hold my hand
And feel the pressure lurking there
Feel emotion bubble up
Pour it in your champagne cup

Let's toast the world,
Or toast the song,
Melodies that linger on
From Sinatra and his New York
If only songs could really talk!
But they can! I know it's true
Look into my eyes so blue,
Although they're brown, (or sometimes red),
The eyes, they tell the truth, it's said.
They tell of sorrow, show forlorn
But I don't intend to moan
I'm happy when I'm on the stage
To sing it high, and deep and low.
Songs from Whitney, Billy Jo,
Celine Dion, Liza Minelli,
Even crazy family Kelly!

And all the others from the telly.

High heels clacking, all that stuff,
Turquoise nails and stulpen cuff.

If I sing I want to see
Hair on your back stand up for me
And be so cold from emotion pure
Music is a lovely cure
For loneliness, for all mankind
In music you can always find
A friend stay with you till the end
Each tale of woe – and so
Enjoy the rhythm, let yourself go!

So I sing it on the stage, you see,
Just for you, and just for me.

6 STRESS

Stress can get you in a mess
Sweating hands, no more or less
Than feeling faint
And tired too
Feed the dog and clean the bird
All these things seem so absurd
When your time is really tight
Try to go with all your might.
Out of breath and wondering who
Will grey my hair next –
Is it you?

The shadows all surrounding me
Of darkest depths, or fantasy?
They make me nervous, make me sad,
Make me want the youth I had
Once in the womb, no more, alack,
Can't bring infant feelings back.
That was secure, no need to fear,
But now the worry's always here.
Falsely figures telling lies
Black beasts beckoning with their eyes.
Moans and groans, cries and sighs,
Wish to wake-up and be wise
To other people wanting more
Of me than I would wish to give.
Longing for in peace to live
Without snatching time – got no time.

Sorry honey – got no money.

Wouldn't it be nice, I know
Time on my hands, no place to go
Time for coffee, and a bun
Filled with cream, and lots of fun.

7 MY SONS

My sons – two
A story true
Of boys with bats
And big fat rats
Table-tennis, football round
Tennis racket on the ground
Ballroom dancing, later date
Bronze, silver gold medallion state
Meeting Nina there in dance
Since then, he is in a trance.
She is the big love of his life
So he made her to his wife.

The other boy, six years younger than
The first. Oh, I love him too.
Both boys they are solid grown
They are beauty, love, for me
All that sons are meant to be.
They criticize me, make me mad.
Do all the things when boys are bad.
But I, a mother, can excuse
Their wildly ways, and their abuse.
I know they love me, love me true,
And I love them, they know it too.

8 A WORK OF NATURAL ART

It's great! It's great!
So don't be late
To keep our date
As I would hate
For you to miss
This wondrous bliss.

The tallest tree
The evergreen.
The longest leaf
I've ever seen.
The smallest stone
That you could see
Bringing out the best in me.
The greenest blade
The bluest hue
The greenest green
Gets greener too
When you are near enough to see
The color lurking in that tree.

So don't be late
Although I'll wait
For you to come
And share with me
All nature's gifts
And rarerity
Spilling colours excessively

Perceiving eyes spontaneously
Lapping up the luxury
Giving oh so generously.

Within the woods
Within the sphere
Packing out their presents here
One o leaves, with form and shape
One of branches spreading out
One of yellow daffodils
Already on the way to sprout.

What a wood! Oh what a dale!
Oh what a pretty fairy tale
Little lads with tulip tops
Little buds with long fruit drops
Little lasses dancing there
In the wind without a care
Time is what we need right now
Time to kiss the calf and cow
Collect the cub and shake the bough
Plant the shrub and feed the sow.
Nip the bud, and wonder how

It came about, this work of art,
So – I think we'd better start –
Time right now to get the plough,
Plant the seeds and milk the cow.

9 MY CAT EDGAR

A booming boy
My pride and joy
Fighting fit my funny toy
I love my cat,
And he loves me
(If he's got his food, you see.)

That's the only thing he asks
No other claim, no strenuous task
He's black, and big with porky chops
You could compare him with a mops.

But he is prettier I would claim,
And by the way – Edgar's his name.
The boys they call him "Eddie louse".
And I, I call him "Mick the Mouse".
Or Mickey Mouse, but there's no fame
In giving cats a funny name.

A cat's a cat, and that is that.
A cuddly coat, so warm to stroke
I let him in, he rushes by
Looking for a juicy pie
Or something more that cats adore
A munchy mouse about the house
A lovely bone to make him moan
And lick his lips and hear him groan.

Oh my cat, my Tom, my leisure
Lolls amongst his cushion treasure
He is the most - my pot of pleasure.

10 THE LOST SOCIETY
(Verlorene Gesellschaft)

How can people be so chill
Cold and daft
And fit to kill
Putting people in a row
To pelt with pellets – go go go
Bang their bullets in your head
Blood is seeping from the dead.

How can they be so hard of heart
Never wanting a new start.

I think these people suffer bad
Their early days were not so glad
Struck with terror and with threat
I wonder if they ever met
A loving person for their heart
To give them that longed-for brand-new start.
A caring person for their needs
To help them on to friendly deeds
To help them love their neighbour first.
No, I'm afraid, we have been cursed
By all these humans, people who
Have hating hearts and wicked ways,
Their head's a horror, all amazed,
They will not see through better days.
A horrid haze, a dreary daze
Walking round and round the maze

To let the rays of sunlight in
But I don't think they'll ever win.

Society will not allow
Its people be content right now
Corrupt and bad and nothing good
Psychotherapy if only it could
Soothe and ease the worlds' disease.

No, I do not think it's time,
It is not here, it's gone.
Society's lost, -
goes on and on.

11a LEOPARD LADY I

One day she'll slink right through the door
Flaunting spots, giving a roar!
Long white claws upon her paw.
Such a sight you never saw,
Holding us lot all in awe,
Lady Leopard, that's the score.

Eddie's[1] getting very jealous
He thought he was her big love in life.
Now he has to sport some spots
Upon his jacket all his life
To get attention from his mother
He says: "Thought there'd never be another
Cat or bat or aristocrat
To take my place, I'll have none of that!"

He sighs and finds a pot of paint,
To paint on big round spots.
His lady sees him doing this – dot, dot, dot.
Oh come here Mick[1], you know your mine,
There's no one else so furry fine
Only you, don't give a fig
for my Leopardy fashion gig.

I love my Leo, so much is true,
But no.1, it's only you.
Forget my jackets with their spots
And all my tights with all those dots,

So Mick, he wipes his spots away,
He says: "I never liked them anyway."

And mother Leo lashes out –
A brand-new sort of shoe's come out,
With spots and dots of leopard,
An ankle strap, that can't be bad.
She puts the shoe on, oh looks great,
And she doesn't hesitate to find her leopard attire

Leo specs, and Leo cuffs, Leo shawls and Leo muffs.
Leo leggings, she's got the lot!
Leo boots and Leo shoes with these she'll never have the blues.
She puts them on, she's feeling free
In all her costume finery.

Then she looks for Mick[1], her cat, gives him a hug.
You're my only one true tiger, love.

---

[1] Eddie/Mick, nickname for Edgar, Karen's cat

11b LEOPARD LADY II

Her husband comes to take a look
He really cannot understand
This Leopardic lady look
Is getting out of hand.

I will not leave you, that you know,
But! - it's him or me
He's got to go! - This Leopard look,
This seed you've sown.
If he doesn't go, I feel prone
To feed you daily with a bone.
Or send you to a place unknown,
Where more exotic leopards roam.

12 A SWEET TOOTH

Cup-cake, twin bake
Butter scotch or pie.
Christmas Pud, if you would
Marshmallow in the sky.
Sip the juice of raspberry fool
On the loose, oh my! Oh my!
Wisps of waffle, crowns of cream
Whipped together, such a dream.
Longing for the taste of toast
With sugar moose and candy bar
Yearning for a greater host
Of chocolate truffles in a jar
Sticky fingers, wonder bar, feeling fit
To dabble in a tray of it
With syrup soft and sauce as well
Such a treat no one can tell
Except me, full of goodies,
What the hell!

13 TWO GOOD REASONS

All my life I've had my breasts
All my life they've been such pests
Wanting to be soft and small
Then again a bigger ball.
What is up? -
So great – so big
Who commentates the fashion swig
Or switch to big and then to small
Fashion fidgets – cannot have them all.

Cupped in lace and silk and so
Throned so warm and all aglow.
Crouching there day in day out
Just itching to get out and about.
These little waddling waggling mounds
An ounce or two complete compounds
Then filled with milk, so full; so rich;
All meant for that tiny titch
A toddling tot who needs the breast,
He sucks and puts them to the test.

All my life I've had my breasts,
And they've been the very best!

14 THE SOLO DANCE

Dancing – having such a ball
In my home, in my hall.

I have no one to dance with me
(I think I'll have a cup of tea).
Then I'll go on dancing high
Touch my toes, then touch the sky.
I like to dance, the feelings grand
Dancing all about the land.

If only I could do it right
I have a dancing partner plight
For no one understands in me
The need to dance, this ecstasy.
If I phone a man, or more,
To dance with me upon the floor
They think the trick is, if they wait,
They'll have me after on a plate
To jitter bug that nasty floor
Take me as they did before.
See me waiting on the ground
Just to take my little hand
Lead me to the bedroom suite
Same old story – am I beat?

You cannot jitter bug around
With all the men, in all the land.
They think your theirs for them to take

Served up on a dancing plate.
They think you are their little treat
After all that dancing heat.

A solo dance I'm in a trance
I dance about without a glance
Into my mirror on the wall
Feeling I have grown quite tall
Dancing solo after all.

I'll stick it out, I'll stay alone
Dancing in my tiny home
Instead of dancing halls so great,
A dance for me – without a mate.

15 A MORBID MONTH

A morbid month, a dismal day,
Though the snow has gone away.
All is dark and dim and cold
Wet and nasty, makes you old.

16 THE BONNET

She's got a little hat,
It's just a tiny bonnet.

It's got a little sprig
Of lavender upon it.

She wears it in the Spring,
And in the summer too,

A great big bow accompanies it
On her rendezvous.

If a man should just perchance
Snatch a fleeting flaunting glance,

Boldly then to advance –
(If he thinks he stands a chance).

This Missy in her bonnet.
The ending of my sonnet.

17 PINK CHAMPAGNE

My pink champagne it is the best
Full of bubbles full of zest.
Floating in a glass so tall
Popping in a bubble ball.

A champagne brunch a luxury
It is the very best for me
Swimming with my Rooibos tea
Toasted crumpets, honey glee
Chunk pork chops and chutney cheese
I'd like some more, if you please
Of that gorgeous Cheddar cheese.
Not too much, I feel at ease
Even if you hear me wheeze.

I drank my drink and ate my peas
Now... Just give me a moment,
If you please.

I want Champagne right out of the pot
 - Oh darling, that is not a lot!
Just another little drop
I've nearly gone over the top.
Can't hold my glass
I'm fading fast
This bubbly drink
(Oh, what a farce!) But
The party's going well, at last.

But now I think I have to go
And sit a while and dream or so.
The pink champagne
Is getting me
The pink champagne
Is all I see –
It's running right away with me!

Bubble blurge – Don't drink a lot.
The pink champagne is all I've got.

No more champagne? - Oh, what the heck.
Grab a glass   And pour out Sekt.

18 TINY TOT, A GIGGLING GIRL, ODE TO EMILY

Tiny tot, a giggling girl
Swishing sashes, swirls and twirls.
Lots of cuty curly curls.
To be a sweetie giggly girl,
Dressed in shiny silver pearls.
Bangles dangling on her feet,
She's such a doll,
A little treat.

Daddy's apple of his eye,
Sweetie wants some crumble pie.
She's wrapped him round her little finger,
She knows it too,
And so does he.
Who cares, so what –
That's how it is.
The family's fit
So closely knit,
And mummy loves her little girl.

The dice is thrown.
The family is together grown.

19 A NEW ROOT - ROUTE

See a new root
Help us on.
Where's the old root?
Gone, all gone.

See a new route
Lead us on.
Engulf the road,
Till then, anon.

An old root withered
Lost and torn
Dried up in the earth forlorn.

And the new route flowing fast
We'll be there soon
God trust and cast
A guiding light
On all that's past.

Leave the withered root to die
Sinking in the darkened sky.

We're getting there
When all is done.
We'll raise our head
And kiss the sun.

Such a dozy dismal doom
Written black upon my tomb.
I have no time
(Quite true, I fear),
My dismal tomb is getting near.
No time left for life,
Oh dear!

A dried up root
Gives not a hoot –
But, what's this coming?
Toot! Toot! Toot!
 Give way, here comes a brand-new shoot.

20 A FAIRY QUEEN

A fairy Queen
All pink and green
And blue and black
And here she is, she's coming back

And bouncing free
Oh jolly, gee,
She's full of love
This turtle dove
Catches kisses,
Cakes and wine.

Full of fancy, so divine,
With lots of ruffles
Velvet, lace.
Swarovski crystals
All in place.

Black lace gloves
And cute big eyes
Lashes lurking in disguise.

A smile here –
A laugh over there
A dangling bow
In locks that flow.
A sparkling sprudling saucy Queen
A fairy too

A slinky slice
Of what's taboo.

To keep her down
Don't even try
Glue her in   -
She'll up and fly.

To lovely lands
That warm her heart,
Looking for a quicker start.

She's chocolate prone,
But what the heck.
A tart or two
Will never do
To spoil her form
Of slender art.

Hearts and thistles
Sun and rain
See her plans go down the drain.

No! No! No!
Not this Queen
Go and bring her back again.
Taking from her bag, a dream
Marking truly what has been.

She's still the top
She's still the cream
Strawberry whipped
This fairy Queen.

Kweenie Karen
Is her name
Loving life, whatever came
She shouldn't have to take the blame,
For things she did, it's not a shame.
She's done it now, and had the pain.

You can't say that
She lived in vain.

21 A PINK PUFF [2]

A pink puff   Fluffy stuff.
Thinking pink   She takes a drink
In her mink and muff.

A pink puff   Soft, not tough.
Floating on a cloud, by guff!

A pink puff   Bold enough
Flying, floating, feather stuff.

A pink puff   By jove, by juff.
End this poem –
Enough's enough!

---

[2] This poem was to be published in my first book, in 2009. As it wasn't finished at the time, I am including it now in this book.

22 THE PINKEST PUFF

Here she comes
Our singing Queen.
The pinkest puff
You've ever seen!

23 FAMILY REUNION

All the family comes today
Tom and Jerry, Keith and Kay.
Step out the car, into the hall
Family reunion, what a ball.

Coming in to meet the brood,
All the babies, and the food.
All the goodies, all the aunts,
All the kiddies have a dance.
Grandma in a sort of trance.

Wait a minute –
Where is Tom? Where is he, where?
 There he is, right over there.
Under the table, eating custard[3], I fear.

What! Wait a bit, are my eyes clear?
He's mixing it with mustard [4], dear!
Why, then that, this nightmare child!
 It's for the cat, (so I've been told).

Oh, this cruel boy!
I must find Mick.
My cat won't be a toy you've picked.
To give Mick mustard, what a trick!
And mixed with custard, oh, no no!

We'll make Tom eat it.

Come here! Don't go.
Want it here,
Or wrapped, to go?

And little Julie, on the ground
Playing with a doll she's found
From Kay, and making not a sound.
Kay is coming now, you know.

And seen her doll
And wants it back.
Goes up to Julie – smack! smack! smack!

Julie's crying, doll is flying
Kay is running off in fear.
Doesn't want to get a whack herself
For coming up too near.

The cats are clawing,
Uncle's snoring,
Joey's looking for a sweet.
Mother's baking,
Auntie's taking
All the plates for the next treat.

What a family, what a hectic
Gaysome gathering, is this crew.
What a way to spend a day.
Can't take much more, I'm all in – pfuh.

[3] Vanille Pudding
[4] Senf

24 BIG MAX

Big Max won't pay his tax.
He saves his "dough"
For tiny Mo.

Mo's his wife
She loves her life.
For this she needs a lot of money.
That's okay,   says Max.
No problem honey.

I'll milk the cow
And sow the seed.
Squeeze all juice from human need.
We need it more,
They need it less.

For Mo, I'll only buy the best.
His underdogs can't pay the flat –
Haven't got the dough for that.
For rent and bread and milk and heat,
The money's lacking, they are beat.

But Max, he makes them pay, no doubt,
Otherwise they're out! out! out!
Of flat and home, then on the roam
To cold and hunger, they are prone.

Big Max, he sits with little Mo,
In his mansion, cocktails in a row.
His round full-face, all aglow,
And bank book he must always clutch,
And his stomach – very much.
And his stomach – very fat
Like Mo's gems upon her hat.

What a couple, what a story,
They have won, and wallow in glory.
But time will tell, the tax man's mad,
The judge thinks Max, his chance has had.
They take him off, in chains, and scoff.
The people clap, (Max in a huff).

Sitting in her mansion home –
Little Mo, all alone.

25 MARY MARY

Mary, Mary, fussy fairy,
How does your garden grow?
Do pansies spright
With such delight,
All in a straight long row?

And the bees come out of the trees,
And suck the pollen dear?
And tulips gay and other bulbs
Come each and every year?

Well, says Mary, a bit contrary,
My garden's not so good.
Every year I plant my seeds
But all I get are lots of weeds.

26 A NICE TUNE

Doodle dum
And dum de doo
What a lovely tune for you.

Hooty hoot and
Hawty hor,
Spinning melody galore.

Whicky wok and
Woddle wum.
Big brass base
Goes tum tum tum.

Bimsy bong and
Doodle dee
Play it till it`s
Time for tea.

Chicka chak
And chooky choo .
No time even
For the loo.

Wicky wacky
Doodle doo
Another little tune
For you.

Wicky wacky
Doodle die
Don't forget to eat
your pie.

My oh me and My oh my.
Hope this tune Won't make you cry.

With wicky wacky
Dicky doo,
Now I have to
Visit the loo.

With so much
Wicky wacky woo
Who's gone wacky –
Me or you?

27 SHE IS BONKERS [5]

She is bonkers
I am sure,
Don't let her in
Beyond the door.

With all her thoughts
And crazy dreams
She's really not
Just what she seems.

She raves right on with all her schemes.
Wanting what she has not got
And what she's got is not a lot.

If you follow her campaign
To bask in sun
And sip champagne –
Lots of money down the drain,
Never bring it back again.

She wants and grabs
And takes and stabs
And bills and coos
For all her dues
To get on where
She wants to be.

She's loveless, rotten
Can't you see.
Her money grabbing fingery.

She hates and waits and goes on dates
And never ever hesitates
To make a match that's good for her.
To see it hatch oh really! Sir!
You don't believe those awful lies
All her would be tender sighs.
She can always tantalize
Lifting up those lovely eyes.
Perhaps it's time you realize
Not too late –
Go in disguise.

---

5 bonkers: verrückt

28 THE CONQUER GAME

She is bonkers[6]
Playing conkers[6]
At a midnight hour.

She is bonkers
With her conkers
But I never tell her so.
For when I need a little cash
She gives me then a little dough.[7]

Wins her cash
By playing conkers,
Not so bonkers,
No! no! no!

---

[6] bonkers: verrückt, conkers: chestnuts
(Kastanien)
[7] dough - money

29 MESSY TESSY

Messy Tessy
Messy Tessy
Messing up the house you see.
Collects her feather boas three
Three for her and none for me.
Only hers, no one should see.

Messy Tessy
Hoarding baskets, cake tins, caskets
Food in bins and other things.
What a mess all should not see
Only for her eyes should be.

What a way to waddle through
The stones, the sticks, the sequins too.
All for art, not all in vain
She uses them again and again.

Christmas papers, silver gold,
Sparkling ribbons, they're not too old
To use again and decorate
A picture or a card of late.

Boxes tumbling to the floor
Feathers floating to the ground.
Feathers floating all galore
Beads and bobbles, please, no more!

Numbering many, (more than a score)
 - What's she using all those for?

Boxes full up to the brim,
Drawers holding all within.
Tins exploding, are they mouldering?
Sometimes she asks
What's lurking in that box?
Or this, or that? There too?
There's such a lot
You cannot view -
I wonder – can we
Make them few?

But give away?
I could no not,
I really think I need the lot!

Feather floater on the ground,
Making not the slightest sound.
All those things, what are they for?
- A very good cause - That's for sure.

Don't come too near
And bark at me
You're barking up
The wrongest tree.
I need my things
I need my stuff
All of it is good enough

To paint and glue
And cut and stick
And paste some on
All so quick.
The leaves, the flowers
In a twirl
Go on for hours
In a swirl.

With all my things,
I love them all.
To be a messy
All in all
Is really not so nice, I'd say.
If people come –
You bid them in another room,
Not full of hay
And hamster ways
(Or bid them just to go away).
Saving things for better days.

I'd like to see my table clear
But not so easy, that I fear.

Messy Tessy
Tales of woe
Can't you let your hoarding go?
Before it ruins up your life
Throw them out, you'll have no strife.

My clothes, they number more than four.
They're falling out the wardrobe door.

My partner cannot understand
His ways are order
In the land –
Quick clear up, so underhand!
His nimble fingers quick to pick
At all my things, my little tick.
Time will tell
If I will be
A better messy, set me free
From all the things that anchor me
In one tight spot
A sightly lot
Accumulating company.

I love my things they love me too
The beauty of a silver hue.
Pink papers dotted all about
So long as they just do not sprout!
My partner would begin to pout,
Although he does that now, you know.
A messy will just have to go. (He says).

The worrying ways of messy life,
With all that colour and that strife.
Picking up what you MIGHT use
But it only brings abuse –
And leaves me in a daze.

The people want a table clear
(Give THEM room to clutter, dear!),
Instead of décor, all in sight,
A table full, to my delight,
Wetting all my appetite.

Messy Tessy there you go,
Asking her to up and throw
Her things so far away.
Perhaps she'll manage it someday.

A messy tries, but all in vain
To put things straight, and back again.
The blockage there from her childhood –
The reason why she can't be good,
Or perfect, as she'd like to be.

Even so –   Can you still love me?

30 MORBID   MONDAY

Morbid Monday
Who wants Monday
After Sunday?
Back to work
And grumps and gruel.

Who wants Monday
After Sunday
Petrol problem
Got no fuel.

Up so early
With the birdy
Down in the dumps
With larger lumps
Of work to do -
I've got the grumps

I loved Sunday
Good old Sunday
Breakfast in bed
The paper I've read.
Coffee going round my head
A croissant, or a bun instead

Tried to telephone with Ted
But I fear the phone was dead
So I'll try to phone old Fred.

Sunday's gone
Oh what a bore
Monday's there and
So much more
All the things I have to do -
Chore after chore.
So now I'll see the day right through

Go on living for a few more days, till
Tuesday, Wednesday, and three more
Hover past me through the door.
Who wants Monday after Sunday?
But then – it's Sunday just once more.

Coffee cream, the days a gem!

31 MY CAT HAS GOT THE FLU

Micky Dicky dicky doo
My cat has gone and got the flu.
I'm wondering now
Just what to do

My little cat
My big fat rat
It cannot catch
A thing like that!

An awful thing to do –

Give a cat the flu.

I think she also has some fleas.

Some FLEAS! Oh no!
No please.
My cat, alright,
Could catch the flu,
But fleas, no this would never do.

Honestly, I'll say to you
I wouldn't know what I would do
With fleas, no, please,
Let him sneeze
Or have a wheeze
After sitting in a breeze,

But never never
FLEAS – you tease,
My cat indulges not in these.

32 BASH the BOYS

Hit on the head
Bash on the bonze
As long as we can get response
To all our questions and our feeling.
Instead of realing,
Ever dealing packs of cards
Beer, a sip,
Or off on a football trip

Let a lady give a tip –
You men don't really know what's what
You have a wife but she is not
A thing to put aside you see
The game is up with loving me.
Yourself put first that's not a lot.
Think of all the things
You've got with her
But they are lost, I know
It's time to go
And bill and coo with other birds.
Each night you have
This sickly plan of loving you.

Your wife is waiting at the door
Wondering if this is all, not more.
A lovely life   a super plan
Married now to such a man.
But careful!   You will wake one day,

Then the farmer's wife   Is making hay
Enjoy the good life   day to day
He'll sit at home   And wonder why
She's turned her back   he'll wait and cry.
She'll sip the drink   and toast the host
With her life she'll make the most.

Yes! That's the way It has to be
When he is bad, not nice to me.
We could have had it oh so good
We could have had it so divine

But now?

How it is – I think it's fine!

33 MY FISH RONALD

I have a fish
A dainty dish!
Oh no, I do not wish
To eat this fish
Of mine, so fine.
I trim his nails
And comb his hair
Brush his teeth
(When my cat's not there.
As he would be jealous!)
Give him food – make him fat.
No! my fish is
Having none of that.
He's modern, fashion wise somehow
Sunglasses sitting on his brow
Wears a cap and bright blue tights
Wears a wrap on winter nights
Dances in his water world
To disco sounds with all the girls
He finds behind a shell or stone
Not wanting once to be alone.
He loves his life.
A super wife
Would be a treat,
Can't be beat.
Those winter nights
To cuddle in
Sometimes my fish

Makes such a din.
But I don't mind
With all of this.
My fishy friend
Is such sweet bliss.

34 NOT TIME TO GIVE UP

I love my life   I love my life
But most of all   I love my wife.

Oh come on now, That is not true
If anything, you just love you!

How could you say things so bizarre
Leave the things just where they are.
I don't love you   You don't love me
That's the way it seems to be.

For years, we've even lost the tears
No more wrangling, fighting, fangling.
Watching all the puppets dangling.

Fight and fuss
No more for us
Just an empty room – a cat,
There's really not much more than that.

What has happened to us two?
30 years of being who
You really didn't want to be.
This is not the life for me.

But much too late the time has come
To sum it up when all is done
And all is said

I may just as well be dead.

But no, I have some more to see
My sons are doing well you know.
Yes, I have some things to do
A poem piece, a picture too.

To sing is also my delight
As long as I can get it right
And bash it out
And bash it well
I'll sing some more
Yes, what the hell!
My life is not quite finished yet –

Off to New York, in a jet.

35 SOPPY BOY

Soppy boy, oh soppy boy
Thought you'd use me as your toy

Tempting me with something good
Thought I would do all I could

With your roses and white lies
Hardly bother to disguise
The things you do,
The things I see
Going on just hurting me.

Silly lad, grotesque fool
But you are not quite so cool
You really thought I'd be your tool
To toss and flick and throw around
Find me lying on the ground.

You poor chap, a sadly heap.
Afraid I have no time to weep.

I must go to other things
Dainty diner dinnerings
Floppy hats and chitter chats
Big fat cats lie on the mats
Bobbly bangles I shall wear
Twinklers sparkling in my hair.

Oh! I do look good, I see,
Never knew who I could be!
Soap and perfume, all that fuss
To make me looking glamorous,
Now I'm off to have some fun
Bye bye baby, the day is done.

36 THE TWIT

Allegation, lamentation
Raging up in aggravation the party pauper
Now he's in the problem zone
Law and order – all alone.
See the party pauper sit
Wishing that he had some wit
To tell a tale
For laughs and screams
He must fight with other things –

Like drinking beer
And being loud (but only when he's in a crowd).
Then he's really
Fighting fit
But – where's his wit? (where ever is his wit?)
Has none of it.
Truth be known –
He's just a twit!

And the end of this sad tale
Sits in jail
Await his bale.

Are we sorry? Not at all!
For this, he took his toll.

37 DIXIE DAISY

Baby baby
Silly crazy.
You're my little
Dixie Daisy.
Making them go crazy, lazy.
You're my little honey pet
My dream come true
Now don't you fret
If I send you home alone
To a world that's quite unknown
I cannot keep you here you see
You cannot stay right here by me
My world's not yours
It's made for me.

Digging, dancing, ever prancing
Now I see you start advancing
Up my little garden way
That is how you came to stray.
Lovely little snicky snail
Go on home and tell the tale
Of where you've been
My little pet
And mention me
And don't forget
To tell them
What you did
And who you see

(And don't forget to mention me)
 And remember, next time come in for tea.

I needn't fret
My snaily pet
Will come again
I'll take a bet.

38 DANCING TIME

Whisking, spinning
Running round
I can hardly see the ground.
Moving grooving to the beat
Hard to follow
Tapping feet.
My partner swirls
And curves and rives
Now he wants to do a jive
A jitter bug, well that's alright
Flamenco? I'm still holding tight.
A Paso Doble is the one
Where I falter; but have fun.
He's got such fire in his feet
Gasping now with every beat
I will hold on -
I love to dance.

A belly dance -
A little prance
Around the floor
Perhaps no more -
Oh! He's off again
For sure.
Here a waltz, tango, and a trot,
Now I think we've had the lot!

39 FIGHTING SPORT

Stays at home
Isn't fit
Just computer – sit! sit! sit!
Doesn't go to sporty grounds
Doesn't try to fight the pounds.

All I do is eat eat eat
Suffer from the hotly heat
(Like this I cannot fight the pounds)
But sport it isn't really fun
I'd prefer to
Eat a bun
With cream inside,
A coke as well.

Listen now, time will tell
I won't dwell.
 On why sport just gives me hell.
I sit at home
I am not fit
Exhausted
Just to think of it.

40 "IT'S DEAD", SHE SAID

All the little do's And don'ts.
All the little wills and won'ts.
Paved your way before with me
Think of you and think of me.
Slapping out the honesty
Can't go on like this you see

I don't love you, you don't love me.
Now I've said it out so loud -
Written down, a dark black cloud.
Just a bit of honesty,
I don't like you, you don't like me.

Where has all the love gone to?
Run away? It must have flew
Right out the window on a dismal day
Blobs of black   and groping grey.
Why'd it have to go astray
Answer this - I couldn't say.
Perhaps it might come back -
It's on it's way!
NO, this I don't believe I'm sure
It's never been so bad before.

The understanding, feelings gone.
Nothing left to help us on.
Relationship that's built on nil,[8]
All gone bad, we've had our fill.

We fight and jab   and want to kill!
Aggression, that is not a laugh,
Cut each one of us in half.

Come, we have to end this stress
It's gotten to a rotten mess.
Give it up, we can't go on
Singing this distressing song.
All the woe And all the wee -
Waiting to get back at me.
Let alone, no use, no more.
You see me walking out the door.

Pink is pink and grey is grey
I haven't any more to say
We'd better stop, call it a day,
Washing all the tears away.

_____

8 nought, nothing

41 UNDERNEATH THE CHRISTMAS TREE

Underneath the Christmas tree
Looking at those presents
What are they all going to be
Looking fine and all wrapped up
All the others gather round
Drinking from their Christmas cup.
I want a watch, Daniel a machine pistol.
Nina's got some nice perfume
In a jar of bright crystal.
Peter always gets the same,
Chocolate with an orange taste,
Dodo likes a silver ball
Not too big and not too small.
All the Christmas paper waste
Karen wants to save in haste -
Before it's gone and thrown away
She hides it for another day
To make her cards and razz ma tazz.
All good things that messies have.

All these presents under the tree
Waiting to be grabbed in glee.
Stephen has the situation clear
He gives the presents s-l-o-w-l-y
Slowly dear!
One for Gert, and Daniela,
(I think she wants an umbrella).

One more present under the tree,
For whoever could this be?
We all have ours, that is said.
Our Edgar's holding up his head
And looking round
And looking buff
They've forgotten me! he thinks,
Oh jolly gee, oh jolly juff.
Aren't I really good enough
For this family feast and stuff?

He falters forward
Wants to go
(He thought that we all loved him so).
While he's making for the door
The family shouts all in a roar,
"Eddie, don't you go away!
There's one more present
Come and stay.
This one's for you, our darling cat".
What is it then?
- A big fat rat!

Oh such relief for Eddie boy
He plays around with his new toy.
Then settles on his cushion bed
The others want to eat instead.
Juicy scrumptious Christmas pud
I'd eat some too it's understood
If I really only could.

But I am full of Christmas glee
Sitting here beside my tree.

42 THE WANTING SONG

Chicky dicky dicky doo
Always wants to bill and coo.
(Think somebody's after you).

Always wants to shimmy shake
Even though your arms do ache.
Always wants to go and stop
In the middle of a shop.

Always wants to eat a lot
Say that you can never stop.
Always wants to fly so high
Sore away up in the sky.

There is nothing I can do
You want and want, it's really true.

I would never tell a lie
Cross my heart and hope to die.

What am I to do with you?
All this wacky wanting to.

It makes me tired, makes me blue.
Come in now and have some stew.

43 COFFEE CAFÉ

Come and have a coffee
Perhaps a tasty toffee?
In the café that we love
"Extra Blatt" or "K & K" [9]
Go inside on a rainy day.
Don't you smoke that pipe, my love
No smoking here! Sorry my dove.

---

[9] kuk: Café in Darmstadt

44 TEA-TIME

Time for toast and time for tea
A tiny tot liqueur, (hi hi!).
Pass around the beans baby,
Don't hog them all, a tune to be
Not all for you, there's some for me.

Sausages and all those pies
What's inside? - It's a surprise!
Dainty little carrot cakes
All the things that mother bakes.

She's done her best to see us fed.
(I think I'll have an egg instead).
Little jam-tarts dancing round
In amongst the salad.

Found some bits of ginger - that I love!
And some shrimps - oh hold on tight!
Not too much, your stomach's full!
I'm not like this usually - as a rule
I count the calories, like a fool.
But this rich and royal spread, ooh!

Eat it up and go to bed.

45 DAUGHTER DAISY

Daughter Daisy
Gone in scorn, and then
Never coming back again.

Hello baby old old lady
Sitting in her "sessel"
Queen-like tressel
Thinks she's someone special.

Bye bye baby old and crazy
Wants to take a walk again.

Hello lady where's your baby
Daughter that you love so long?
Is she really gone?

Daughter Daisy makes you crazy
Gone in scorn - and then?

She's never coming back again.

So you wait, and hesitate
To phone your Daisy gem.

A family fight
Was not alright
A never ending sadly plight.

Hello baby
Old old lady
Sitting in her den -
She thinks of Daisy then.

Old old lady gone half crazy
Goes to take her pen.
Writes her child again.

"Dearest Daisy
Your my baby
Come back home again.
Please write to me of when".

46 OH BROTHER, MOTHER!

Oh no, the party's going fast
Our mother's back (if she can last)
She's jiving, jumping on the floor
She tells the band
To give it MORE!
She jumps and twirls
And spins around
Her curly curls all hanging down
Amongst her pearls and all the girls.

Oh, now what's she going to do
It's just too much for me to chew
Oh no, oh no, said Daniel, quick,
I think she's going to be sick!

For heaven's sake,
Does she think of her back-ache?
And you know, it's getting late.
What shall we do with this wild thing?
Oh no! Now she's getting up to sing!
Singing here and dancing there
Writhing up, the crowd in cheer.
Mother will this ever stop
- Just go home – hop hop hop

Her sons they really are concerned
Stephen shouts "she'll never learn!
Our Tiger Lily's at it again".

All our efforts all in vain.

One foot forward, one foot back
High heels clicking- clickerty clack.
Stephen runs to fetch a seat
She might feel faint or old and weak.
"Oh no, " says mum, "I'll not be beat".

His mother dancing on the floor,
A nightmare now, she's not a bore.
Writhing reeling such galore
Everybody wanting more.
This fairy dairy tippy toe
Stretching up all in a glow.
Mum, you know we love you so,
But don't overdo it though.

The boys are buff
They've had enough
Looking in on one so tough.
They call to Gerhard - "Do your stuff!"
Take her home, put straight to bed
So much jingling in her head.

Singing here and dancing there
Mum looks up - What do you want from me my
dear?
Let me live without a care.
You know I say that, I do swear
There isn't a son most anywhere

Who has to hold it out like here
This bonny bouncing dancing bear.
Singing too, she does the lot
Oh God - now she's off to trot
Flamenco - her speciality.
A rose between her lips with thorn
She'll be going strong till dawn.

Get the sleeping tablets here
Come, have a little sip my dear.
But to her, it's rather clear
Turns it down - thank you, no fear.

How and when's it all to end?
Mother's chatting with a friend.
I don't think it'll end at all
Now she's doing musical.
Mother, (of course), she knows them all
Songs from "Cats", Minnelli's acts,
Go and get her black top hat.
Time for "Cabaret" you know.

We give up, this one's on us
All this nightly music fuss.
Where's Shakira gone this time?
Thinking out a brand new rhyme.
Nina just wants to hear a song from Freddie
Ringing in her ear, Bohemian Rhapsody, my dear.

47 Dr. DAN Is there a MED in the house?

16.11.2014

Feeling sad?
Come over bad?
Worst sore throat
You've ever had?

Need a pill? To keep you still
Liver salts   If you will

No more beer, No more cheer
Can't go on like this my dear

Full of pain, Sick again
All your hopes
Gone down the drain

No more fun
All is done
Give up the gin, and the rum
And don't forget
The big cream bun.

Help, I hope
Is on the way
I need it more
From day to day.
My time has come
There's no more bliss

I really can't
Go on like this.

The help I need
Must now come fast
This awful night
I might not last!

Find the phone
If you can
And get the man
Called Dr. Dan.

48 HUBERT HUK

ehemaliger Kunst Kollege, Hubert Kretschmer, (www.whooshes.de)

Part I   The Nose

He has a hook
Upon his nose.
It's sitting there
And grows and grows.
Why this is, no one knows.

That's the reason he has took
A nick-name - thus
We call him HUK.

Huky hik, huky huk,
Loves it when the ladies look.
Oh darling hooby
They all shook
When eyeing his most handsome hook!

Part II

Mr. Whoosh - The Photographer

Hubert Huk is Mr. Whoosh
Whooshing here, whooshing there
His photos whoosh with lots of flair
The man's a genius, doesn't care
Where his whoosh lands – anywhere.

49 TAPPY TOES

Here comes little tappy toes,
He's the pigeon down the road.
Black and shiny, such delight
He's there each morning
From his flight.
Waiting for a tiddy bit,
Walks right up and has a sit
Upon the window sill a bit.
Lovely tiny tappy feet
Shining eyes
And oh so sweet.
Has his meal
And flies away.
Tomorrow back
And tweeting gay.

50 CARIBBEAN DISASTER March 2009

A Caribbean craving
Caribbean trip
A Caribbean cruise
In the waters take a dip.

I thought I'd have a holiday
Islands all galore
Sunny pipping parrots
Numbering a score
Pecking, popping, peeping,
Making me want more.

Mangos, dangos, coconuts.
Orchids, brilliant colour cuts,
Banana trees and sweet perfume,
Whatever then led to my doom?

A pain! exasperating shock,
I'd never had it quite so bad.
And then, and then, before we planned
To step into the airport plane.
The people gazed, the stewardess gasped,
A doctor please, but very fast!

He said - Between us two you see
I wouldn't step inside that plane, not me!
Instead we two will take a trip
To Frankfurt Clinic, quick! quick! quick!

There your kidney stone will know
What doctors do with stones that grow.
They'll shoot it, mash it up inside
And send it on a longer ride.

So much for Caribbean flair,
The Frankfurt Easter sun will do.
I'll just imagine in my bed
The sun is flowing overhead.
My Caribbean cocktail mix will help me on,
My pain all fixed, my illness gone!

The snow had fallen fast.
Crisp and hard, it looked like
It would last.
The day, turning into grey
From silver white
Disappearing slowly into night.
But onward I still sped inside the wood,
My legs and sticks [10] carrying me
As fast they could.
But then a glossy spot, Just under me,
My feet slid out and ended by a tree.
I tried to get up, stand again once more.
My wrist was painful, broken to the core.
(Oh, what a bore!)
Don't think I can take much more.
What dilemma, What a drag
To taunt me in the snow
I must get up and go go go.
I must get back to face
This mighty blow.
I staggered, waggled, joggled slowly on.
For now, such walking pranks are surely done.

Clutching my hand before
It fell aground
The doctor examined, making little sound.
And then he looked me
In the eye and said: "A plaster case,

And six weeks in your bed".

Disaster came upon me
How could I brave the world with one hand?
No, not I!
Asking myself - how did this happen, And why?
Finding no answer, I then began to cry.

No point in feeling sorry anymore
Get up and face the fact with fine bravour.
This ruined wreck of wrist
This tiny winzy thing you call malheur
Will go in Spring,
Of that I'm sure.

---

[10] Nordic Walking

Pink and sticky
White and sweet
All this stuff
For me to eat.

What a dream
A holy scene
A heavenly treat
This sweetie meat.
All for me!

Clouds of candy
Way up high
Pink and white
All in the sky.

Puffs of pink
A sheer delight
I'll suck them in
These whiffs of white
Now's my chance
So hold on tight.

Ein Wolken Bad
Von pink papoo
I'll eat the lot
Do you want some, too?

A merry mix, A sweet affair,
A gooey fix , A devil dare.

This podgy goo, a treat for two.
This love affair, this tea for two.
Come eat with me - That's IF you dare.
Come eat with me - But be aware
For sweet stuff
Makes you fat and round
Then you will be quite astound
When your clothes no longer fit,
You sit in a chair
And can't get out of it!

Come, you lick and suck
And eat and (what rhymes with suck?)
Come, you slurf and burp and chew,
Swallow and spew.[11]

You eat and eat and if you do
You'll double and become
Two of you!
Or three or four,
Then more and more.
And more ... and more and more and more...

Your feet will cease to touch the ground
You'll take off, flying all around
Like a Michelin X tire man.
Whimpering, simpering, what a sound!

When you can - gasping, breathing quick for air.
Floating in the hemisphere
Moaning - "Fly me out of here!"
I'd like to have a pint of beer."
No! Better not, it's got calories, I fear!

Just like this flossy, fluffy stuff
Leaves you feeling in a huff.
This candy pink, and candy floss
Enough's enough of all this stuff.
I'm looking like a big baboon
Grotesque pig, I'll explode soon.
Gigantic whale, an albatross,
All this candy, all this floss.

A calorie count, I declare war
On this floating beast, this is the score
A rolling ball of FAT galore.

---

[11]kotzen

53 SATTLER'S SEWING

Sattler swinging his scalpel,
Here, and there, oh what the hell

If lines do come, then they will go
Just give him time to cut and sew.

Give him time to form a shape
That ladies like, so fine, sedate.

Give him time to smooth and shine
The lady now can wine and dine

In new attire, what a shape!
Slinky sun suit, brand new cape.

He's done it again! A wonder girl
Full of magic, full of curl.

No lines to see upon her face
No bumpy curves, she's full of grace.

No bulging thighs, or big broad nose
No drooping breasts, want none of those!

No hanging eye lids, spreading waist
Size 36 we're now to taste.

Floating on a dreamy feather
Our Gert gives only sunny weather.

You'll never age when he comes by
You know by now, the reason why.

He keeps his ladies young and slim,
He keeps his ladies ever trim.

What a world of lasting youth,
What a world, but where's the truth?

54 SPOILT BRAT

You show your fist
And raise your voice.
Can't there be another choice?
Quiet, gentle, said with love.
No, not for him, he can rely
On mummy's support, his alibi.
He's her little cutie pie.
He's the apple of her eye.
But how's she brought him up!
Oh why?
Spoilt brat - you can't deny.

55 KILLING TIME   I

Hello Sidney, hello Sue,
Shall we have some tea for two?
Don't let me down
And come too late -
While I wait
I'll have some cake

Milk the cow
Or tank the car.
I'm not really
Getting far.

Let's take a walk
And window shop
Kill some time
Before we stop.
Another coffee?
Sugar pop?

While I'm waiting
In a queue
I'll write my dairy,
Look at you.

Dust the lamp
And clean the floor
Getting cramp
Again for sure.

So much time
To analyze
Time to think
And criticize.

Wondering next
Just what to do.
I could go
And talk to you

Feed the cat
Or play it cool
Enough of that
You lonely fool.

Time upon my hands
For sure
Where's the stress?
Exciting tour?

I can take no more of this.
I want my stress -
My soulful bliss.

All your life
Stress accompanies you
Now you don't know
What to do.

I've paid the bills
And mowed the lawn.
Sewed my dresses
That were torn.

I've picked tomatoes
From the pot.
Sorted saucers, cups, -
The lot.

Now whatever
Can I do?
Cut my nails,
And made the stew.

Too much time's a curse
Or worse.
Why can't it simply let me be!
Oh, now I think
It's time for tea.

56 JAMES, THE COOK (Jamie Oliver)

Jamie Oliver said to me
"A cook I think you'll never be
Ginger in your apple-tea!
Perhaps for you
Thanks - not for me."

(She says)
I've bought your book
So you will see
I'll cook and cook
Just take a look
And what I've made
You'll get for tea.

(Jamie)
"I'll take a look
Alright my dear.
BUT - eat it. Not tonight!
No fear!

Inside your pot
There's not a lot
Of vitamins -
I'd say just Schrott!"[12]

(She says)
"Oh Jamie! Jamie!

I'll never be
A good cook
Of gourmetry."

(Jamie)
"Come to me
In my restaurant den
I'll give you menus
One to ten."

(She says)
"Okay, alright
I'll give up
And eat the goodies
From your cup!

Let me try
A super sip
Of poreé pleasure
In a dip.

Mm! mm
Yes yes, it's good."

(Jamie)
"Well sweet mum
I knew it would.

I'm Jamie boy
The super cook.

O'er all the land
They use my book.

I'm even often on the Telly
For people who just love their belly."

Jamie boy works all the night,
Come inside and take a bite.

---

[12] German for rubbish

57 TEA - BUT NO CAKE !

Hello dear, the pot is on
Crumpets ready, won't be long.
Is Martha coming, Sue and Sal?
All the ladies, all the gals.

Best bone China, out today,
The red ones with the gold rim ray.
All this bother, all this fuss,
Yes, of course, it's all for us.

Serviette and silver spoon,
I'm feeling like I'm over he moon.
Janet will be here quite soon.

Cream coloured roses sitting up
I'll put one by each red bone cup.
The angel cake, the walnut fudge,
If Phyllis dozes, give her a nudge.

Étagère with petit fours.
Linda has her lemonade with straws.
The tea is done, the table's set,
Darjeeling tea is what you get.

Here they come, a merry bunch
Sitting down to munch munch munch.
But - what is this I see? They drink their tea -
But munching, no! they're really slow.

A crumpet Carol ? Or sponge cake?
Cucumber sandwich might you take?
No, she said, and Jane no, too.
"I watch my figure, do not you?
You should you know, you're over weight!
No more juicy carrot cake".

All this fuss, with all this food,
I really think they're being rude!
My time was spent with making, baking.
But the gals, they are forsaking.

All my efforts, all in vain.
Now they're up and gone again.
I, alone at my table sit,
Wondering what to do with it. -

The cakes, the scones, the creamy bit,
Leave it now, and go and knit!
No! I'll drink and eat till all is done.
An iced cake here, a nice cream bun.
Walnut slice, a great big one!

Chocolate chip or lemon dip
Bake well tart or pastry heart.
Next time I won't work to the bone
When the gals are diet prone.
They can sip on cups of tea
But not a crumb they'll get from me!

58 BABY BUNTING

Yes, she has my big brown eyes.
And my dark hair, (lots of sighs).
She smiles so sweetly, we're going wild,
With pleasure - our first grandchild.

But wait - if Stephen has a baby, oh,
That makes me a grandmamma!

She giggles, coos, with all her might,
Waking grandpa up in fright.
She waddles, crawls about the floor,
Loosing panties - and lots more!
Oh baby, what a stinky pooh!
You've done it again, but that is you.

Dear sweetie, tweetie, pot of joy
Playing with her brand-new toy.
Passing pleasure all around
When she's learnt another sound.

Walking, talking, jumping, bumping,
She's our bobble baby bunting.
She's so cute and oh so coy
Zest for living, boy oh boy!

Baby when you're big and grown,
Don't walk too proud, and don't you moan.
Lend an ear for those who need,

Share your lot and don't show greed.

Honest you should be, and more
To those who've fallen to the floor.
Pick them up and help along,
Be modest, and remember this song.

59 AND NOW I'M 60!

It's my birthday today
- hip, hip, hooray!
But what do I say
What do I do?
Festivity and celebration?
I am over half a century.
- Reason to celebrate.
Well, yes, I made it this far!
Not quite sure I'd like to make it through
To a whole century - Would you?

Coffee, champus, lots of wine,
Gateaux, sirloin beef divine.
People say you look just fine
In your pink, and mink to dine!

It's my big day - well so they say.
Wasn't sure I'd want it this way.
So much pomp and so much stress.
Now my hair is in a mess.
Really though, I couldn't care less.

Give a speech, well must that be?
Concentrated all on me.
Tell them how my life began
What I did and what I sang.
Saw it through but couldn't they see
The one thing that I wanted to be

Was a singer on the stage.
Sing my heart out, passion divine.
Giving everyone a cold shudder
Up and down their spine.

What! A singer on the stage!
Don't forget one thing - your age!
Now your 60, now you're fat,
You can't neglect such things as that.

But as I wanted first to sing,
A tiny girl of four I'd been.
Then 15, 16, ! you're too young!"
Your life hasn't yet begun.
School and "A" levels,[14] career, job,
All the things you're thinking of.

All the things I have to do,
All the things I have to be,
Before I begin to think of me.

And now I'm 60 - my happy day,
But where ever did life slip away?

Well, take a glass, let's make a toast
To living life to the utmost.
Live it out and live it in
Live it up, and pass the gin!

Happy Birthday, Karen mate!

Let's hope it isn't much too late
To do your thing - whatever it be.

Singing - painting - poetry.

---

[13] "A" levels   Abitur

60 THE CHRISTMAS TREE

Three branches? No more?
Is that what they're for?
To make a tree!
A Christmas tree?
Complete with needles, and a star?
Is that just what you're looking for?

You will admit it looks quite poor,
Mangy, crabby, not alot.
As other trees it has not got
The pomp and pride and evergreen.
It's rather grey, a bit gangrene.

It doesn't stand so large and tall,
Towering high, right up the wall.
With bangles, baubles, lots of light,
With candy, and an angel bright.

Are you really sure, you bought no more,
Than these three branches tied together
To make a symbol of a tree?
Are you really kidding[14] me?

You can't be serious, (just a thought),
These three branches, really bought
In a shop that sells fine firs.

Such comments...And I suffer so,

It is my tree, I believe so!

My mother brought it home, it's true,
 Three branches tired together,
I wonder if she worried whether
I would be a little distraught
At the sort of " tree" she'd bought?

But when a tiny girl can see
Her mother hasn't more, just me
Then it's alright, it's love you see
That brought the little tree to me.
And as I see, my fantasy will get me through
A better tree could never do
Than this I have - it's really true!

I love THIS ONE, I do, I do!
The only problem is - there's you...
My friends, who shouldn't come too near
At Christmas, when the "tree" is here.
I know they'd laugh, and that's not fair.
If they have got so much to share -
But I'm too proud to beg or moan.
In my poverty I have grown
Quite used to having less than that.
No fine firs green with bows of red.
"Less is more" Jill Sander[15] said.

I like my "tree", enough of that.
Until better days I will see,

Then I'll have a gorgeous tree!

But now that I am bigger grown,
I cannot say that trees alone
Can make you happier, full of fun.
It must, you see, in love be done.
It must, you see, be from the heart,
And if it's not? - A brand new start?

---

[14] machst Du Spass?
[15] Fashion Designer, Mode Designer

61 WHAT'S IN A NAME ?

My cat has many names you know.
I call him Jack, and sometimes Joe.

His proper name is Eddie Maus,
Edgar darling, Edgar Laus.

I call him Mick, or Mack or Mo,
Then always coming back to Joe.

Or Fluffy, Fruity, little boy.
He knows his name, this bundle of joy.

I call him Popsy, when I'm prone.
Or Mopsy, Topsy, he'll not moan.

Takes it as a dog a bone,
As long as I leave him alone.

I wonder -
Has he a name for me?
He doesn't say a lot you see.

It could be mops, or pops as well.
With cats you really cannot tell

Just what they think and how they feel.
Could call me Jack or maybe Jill.

Or lovely Leopard Lady?
No, no, he doesn't go for that.
(He doesn't like a spotted cat).

Perhaps it's Puschel Wuschel Wee,
Perhaps he calls me Dainty Dee.

Or dozy Dora, Flighty Flora.
The names are all okay with me.

As long as we two can fantasy,
A nameless couple - meant to be.

62 THE POT OF STEW

One day I had a little pot
Full of munchy food, the lot.
Chunky meat and crunchy carrot,
Should I pop in the pot, the parrot?
Onions, pepper, for the stew,
On the stove for us to chew.
But first I have to cook it all.

The doorbell rings, a deafening noise.
The postman brings a nice surprise!
I pack it out, and then return
To pot and stove, (it shouldn't burn!)
But where's my pot! And where's my stew?
What is all this coming to!

The cat is looking rather glum.
He licks his lips and rubs his tum.
Oh ! You bad boy, you've had the lot.
- My stew, all in my little pot!

63 KILLING TIME   II

If you have some time on hand
The feeling used to once be grand.
But when you have it more and more
You start to wonder what it's for.

Time used to run and run and run,
Sitting underneath the sun.
Now it's slower than a snail,
Makes me bored and want to wail.

Counting seconds, minutes, hours,
Sitting watching wilted flowers.
I want to jump right up and run,
(Or sit down first and have a bun.)

Goes on like this my time will come.
These days, these years, my time is done.

64 THE JOGGING SONG

Jog jog jog jog jog jog jog

```
j           g    j
 o        o      o
   g     j          g
```

I want to jog, I really do!
I have to jog, it's really true!

I must   j - o - g

It's sitting on my hips,
It's creeping in my toes.
It's running up my neck
And even down my nose.
Everywhere it goes!

This FAT of mine, I need it not.
It grows and grows
It's such a lot!

It's in those chocolates, biscuits, truffles.
Trying to hide between the ruffles
Of my evening dress, oh dear!
It cannot hide, it's coming near
And near and nearer.
The situation is getting clearer.

So much fat, and so much fuss,
I think of fat instead of us.
I think of form and being slim
My hope is starting to get dim.
My only dream is being small -
I wish I could forget it all!

But no! To jog jog jog jog jog jog jog.
Don't get fat or be a hog.
And don't get lazy, I have to be a dainty daisy.
A thinly miss, a slimly girl
To make the men go in a twirl.
Turning heads at me the girl
Who's slim and nice, has no vice,

Except the passion for a jog
And sport and sport and sport again,
Running till I don't know when.
Running till I don't know how.
Panting, puffing, sweating brow.
Forgetting that the moment´s NOW.
To live and love, and EAT, enjoy.
Accept the form that's really me.
It's always there if you can see
That's the fact that has to be -

Accept yourself, for that's the key.

65 NORDIC WALKING (Ode to Hans & Renate)

Nordic Walking, talking talking,
This is the sport that's meant for me.
A jabber[16] here, a natter[16] there,
In the group without a care.
We walk and walk, and talk and talk,
And swirl those sticks, fantastic mix
Of laughter, conversation pure.
This Nordic Walking, give me more.
It definitely is not a bore.

The trees, the birds, the freshly air,
Marching on if you dare.
A deeply breath, a rosy cheek,
Doing it three times a week.
This style of life can't make you weak,
But strong, and free from colds and flu,
And running to the doctor too.

Oh such a life I strive to have
With Hans, Renate, all the group.
A happy, healthy, hearty troop.
Nordic Walking, so much flair,
No finer group is anywhere
To find within this town, you see.

Yes, Nordic Walking has to be!

[16] jabber

[16] natter. schwätzen

66 FISHERMAN'S PLIGHT

Crabs and shrimps and fish and chips,
Lemon cod, spit out the pips.
Winkles, octopuses too
Full of iron, said my mother.
They keep you slim, they're tasty brother.

Who would have thought that you and I
Would have to give them up for ever,
As all the sea is bare, empty of it's treasure,
And what was lurking there.
Because the human species are such greedy pigs
To squeeze all waters' riches out of the ocean wide.
Then take it in abundance, (The last fish tried to hide).

We don't blame the fisherman,
He has to live, we know.
But all the oil tankers,
With oil for all the bankers,
Leaking slicks of tricky black
Making fish, (and birds), so sticky that
They cannot swim, birds cannot fly,
Their feathers falling from the sky.

Birds so black, and fish so filthy
They can't rejoice when they diminish in number
Due to that black gold rush.
In our sea there's just a hush.

No more life. No more food.
Just lots of sticky oily blues.
I loved my haddock and my skate,
But factories pour out their dirty state
Into the once clear water - just stress!

And now we have it - What a mess!
Plastic in abundance, illness too.
The sinners see, but do and do
Their best to beat the battle.

The fisherman's friend is sad,
Nothing left from fish he had
To catch within the limit set.
To give his child a little treat.
Instead of fish, he'll give them meat,
If he can afford that meal.

67 GETTING OLDER

Getting old is not much fun
Greying hair, keep out the sun
Enhances wrinkles coming on

Creams and paints and all that stuff
To stop the skin from feeling rough
What a bore a daily chore
To keep your youth
From looking poor. Alas! It doesn't do much good.
I'm afraid I never thought it would.
You will get old and older still.
Come, it's time to make your will.

Older older you will come
Spend your money till it's gone.

Older, older you will be
Most likely that they all will see
Your bloating tum, your double face
Chins falling all over the place.
Come on, try and do your best.
Erotic nights so full of zest
Aren't the only thing on earth.

Come on, and give it all it's worth!

68 THE TYRANT

They've thrown him out
Of his own house.
This tyrant can't keep
Cat, nor mouse.
Not to mention
Dick, the dog.

You know we don't ask much of you.
- A bite to eat -
- A walk, or two.
A cuddle here, a pat right there
Is all that we require,
- Sitting comfy by the fire?

He didn't buy a bone for Dick,
And me, the cat, I have to sit
For hours, all upon my own -
Waiting till he comes on home.

Oh! the lumpy life we led.
Until we threw him out instead.
Find the kitchen
Fill our belly.
Come on Dick,
Let's watch the Telly!

Short Biography

Born in London, I went to school there, studied English, art and drama, played in several theatrical groups, recorded own records, and travelled to India.

In 1973 came to Germany where I had a record contract with *EMI Electrola*. Was awarded two golden records with the group "*Arabesque*".

I studied art and English, with the main emphasis on painting at the *Johann Wolfgang Goethe-University* in Frankfurt and became a teacher at a private grammar school in Darmstadt, Hessen.

It is 11 years ago that I published my first poetry band, "*The Pink Puff*". Since then I have finished working officially in a grammar school. I have had more time for my own art exhibitions and carried on singing on the stage. Also, I have had more time for travelling, and for photography. I was also a lecturer in the *Volkshochschule* in Darmstadt for several years.

Now at the age of 70 years, I have two sons, three grandchildren and a cat called Lucy. (Edgar died in 2015).